The World-Changing Prayer of Jesus

Unity, Love and the Great Commission

Edward N. Gross

Parson's Porch Books

The World-Changing Prayer of Jesus

Table of Contents

I dedicate this book to the participants of the Fourth Lausanne Conference on World Evangelization (Sept 22-28, 2024) and to their every team of partners that helps them in their devotion to fulfill the Great Commission of our Lord Jesus Christ in our generation.

I also dedicate it to the late Rev. Dr. Juan Carlos Ortiz, who challenged and delighted the attendees of the First Lausanne Conference, in 1974, speaking of the renewal of New Testament discipleship in Buenos Aries, Argentina. His book, *Disciple!* is needed now more than ever.

Unite and help us all, Holy Spirit!

Preface

The Lord focused my attention, in 2011, on how I was off track. Way off track. Although I was a highly trained evangelical missiologist, I did not understand the Great Commission of Jesus Christ! That's like a mathematician not grasping $2+2=4$. So, what did I do when I was confronted by this reality?

By His grace, I humbled myself and repented. I, then, devoted my life to discovering what New Testament Discipleship was. What it meant to Jesus and His 1st century disciples. I reasoned – How can I fulfill His Great Commission to disciple the nations if I do not rightly understand what it means to be a disciple, myself? So, I researched the Scriptures and many books, both Christian and Jewish. My conclusions and applications have been carefully written in several books.[1]

---

[1] Are You a Christian or a Disciple? *Rediscovering and Renewing New Testament Discipleship* (2014); Disciples Obey: *How Christians Unknowingly Rebel against Jesus* (2016); Fruitful or Unfruitful? *Why it Really Matters* (2017); The Amazing Love of Paul's Model Church: *How the Thessalonians became disciples and reached their region with the Gospel* (2017); 100 Days with Jesus: *A Guide to Transformation by Knowing God and Living in His Presence* (2018); The

While doing my research, I discovered that I was not alone! There were many others being led by God to ask the same questions and arrive at the same answers! And, then, I was drawn into the global fellowship of thousands who were seeing the huge gap between today's Christianity and New Testament Christianity bridged – by returning to New Testament discipleship. In God's wonderful providence, we have been united in the miraculous phenomenon known as Disciple Making Movements.[2] The DMMs of today are the most powerful, multiplying, transformational, global Kingdom movements since the book of Acts!

Last year I was privileged to help participate in an emerging DMM in Pakistan, an Islamic Republic where 97% are identified as Muslim. The incredible multiplication, miracles and persecutions there are one of the most

---

Harvest Prayer of Jesus: *Why American Christians are Missing Today's Global Renewal* (2020); Disciple the Nations! *By Peace not Pressure (2023).*
[2] Read about these in Miraculous Movements by Jerry Trousdale; A Wind in the House of Islam by David Garrison; Contagious Disciple Making by David and Paul Watson; Acts and the Movement of God by Steve Addison; Motus Dei by Warrick Farah, ed.; The Multiplier's Mindset by Cynthia Anderson, etc.

remarkable recent stories revealing the unstoppable advancement of the Kingdom of Christ on earth.

The reality of DMMs and their significance in missions is so undeniable that whole denominations and mission agencies are revamping their Great Commission fulfilling strategies to prioritize this renewal. In this book, I am going beyond the reality of DMMs to uncover *how* Jesus wants us to proceed. According to His own words, uttered in the most intimate prayer He spoke to His Father, preserved in the Bible. I have purposely made this book short. Because, what Jesus prayed was crystal clear. So, what I now share with you can be perfectly understood. And powerfully followed. I hope that you will see the emergence of DMMs as an answer to Jesus' prayer, and desire their power to be unleashed in your life and ministry through the person and work of the Holy Spirit.

I have written a short, focused work, so it can be freely downloaded or inexpensively purchased - throughout the world. At first, I intended this to be a rather extensive work which would deal with objections and offer many illustrations. But, instead, I have been led to shorten its message so that the impact might be greater, and it distributed immediately.

Some further discussion on critical issues have been put in the Appendices.

I pray that our Father in heaven will exalt our Lord Jesus Christ, by answering His John 17 Prayer, in our day, through the power of the Holy Spirit.

Edward N. Gross
September 2024

PART ONE

The Prayer of Jesus

Chapter One
The Life Changing Question

It is commonly known, by those who read their Bibles, that Jesus lived a life of prayer. But, let me ask you an important question about His prayers. Be careful to think before you answer this question, because it may both challenge and change your life. And, through you, the world.

Has any single prayer that Jesus prayed on earth been unanswered?

I am asking this of those prayers of His that are revealed on the pages of the New Testament.

This is no trick question. Rather, it is a foundational one. This question, when answered biblically, has transformed His followers, His disciples, today—globally! Let me help you answer this lifechanging question. A look at what He said to the Father about His prayers, at the tomb of Lazarus, gives us the answer.

"… And Jesus lifted up his eyes and said, 'Father, I thank you that you have heard me. <u>I knew that you always hear me</u>, but I said this on account of the people standing

around, that they may believe that you sent me."' (John 11:41-42)

Big or little. Asking the Father to bless His meal, to comfort the sorrowing, to heal the sick, to raise the dead -- Jesus' prayers were always answered by His Father. He said so. So, we can count on it. His prayers have been or will be answered.[3]

Our faith rests on His being sinless. Our salvation depends on His being the unblemished Lamb of God, who *"takes away the sin of the world!" (John 1:29).* John later would insist, *"You know that he appeared in order to take away sins, and in him there is no sin.... The reason the Son of God appeared was to destroy the works of the devil." (1 John 3:5,8).* His recorded and unrecorded prayers made this a reality!

What if I showed you a prayer of Jesus where He requests of the Father how He wants to reach the world and restrain the devil through His disciples? A prayer in which a brief, clear and repeated strategy of worldwide salvation is

---

[3] This is true, even in Gethsemane, when He, under unparalleled pressure and sorrow, cried out, "My Father, if it is possible, let this cup pass from me; nevertheless, not as I will, but as you will" (Matthew 26:39)

revealed and requested by Jesus. It's right there. In your Bibles. Hidden in plain sight. And He mentions you and me as the subjects through whom He wants to work. Why have so few seen this and been moved to act in line with it? Why have we, up to today, been so unconcerned about what Jesus prayed would be done through His Church? Can we consider this and remain unmotivated and unchanged? I don't think so. Help us, Father, fulfill the will of your Son and our Lord Jesus.

Chapter Two
The Astonishing Revelation

What is the prayer of Jesus which impacts global history? These words were heard by the Father as the will of His Son, God incarnate in human flesh. They had to be answered and fulfilled.

This prayer, often referred to as *The High Priestly Prayer of Jesus*, is found only in the Gospel of John. The revelation was given by the Holy Spirit to John. He supernaturally remembered it verbatim and wrote it down for all to consider. I have not revealed it. It's not my revelation. But, make no mistake, I was tremendously blessed to see it and, here, share it. I call it: *The World-changing Prayer of Jesus*. For it is a prayer that directed His destiny and that of His Kingdom: His citizens, His servants, His disciples, throughout human history.

The setting is at the close of our Lord's last meeting with His Apostles before His crucifixion. On the night He was betrayed by Judas and forsaken by them. So, this prayer was uttered within 24 hours of His death. He was in the Upper Room, where he had just washed their feet, intimately spoken with them about what was about to happen, eaten the Last Passover meal, initiated the Lord's Supper and joyously predicted the glorious coming and mission of the Holy Spirit (see John 13-16).

Jesus' entire prayer is recorded in John 17:1-26. Only a small portion of that communion with His Father is in the form of petitions or requests. Single books have been written on this one chapter, for it is the longest and most revealing prayer of Jesus in the Bible. It is a look at the most intimate communication between the Father and the Son in all of the Scriptures. Its importance cannot be overstated and should not be overlooked.

For our purpose, here are the petitions, the requests, within the prayer. I will not speak to the petitions that He made in reference to Himself and to His Apostles. Just read them, learn from them, marvel at them and worship our God through them. We will, rather, pay close attention to those requests which Jesus prayed for all subsequent generations of believers. These words are precious as they reveal the will of Jesus Christ for all His blood-bought children, including you and me, today.

<u>Requests for Himself</u>

• **"…Glorify your Son that the Son may glorify you." (17:1)**

• "And now, Father, glorify me in your own presence with the glory I had with you before the world existed." (17:5)

<u>Requests for His then-present Apostles</u>

• "I am praying for them. I am not praying for the world but for those whom you have given me, for they are yours." (17:9)
• "…Holy Father, keep them in your name, which you have given me <u>that they may be one, even as we are one</u>." (17:11)
• "But now I am coming to you, and these things I speak in the world that they may have my joy fulfilled in themselves." (17:13)
• "I do not ask that you take them out of the world, but that you keep them from the evil one." (17:16)
• "Sanctify them (set them apart) in the truth; your word is truth." (17:17)

<u>Requests for future believers</u> (including us)

• "I do not ask for these only, but also for those who will believe in me through their word, that they may all be one; just as you, Father, are in me, and I in you; <u>that they also may be in </u>us, so that the world may believe that you have sent me." (17:20-21)

• "The glory that you have given me I have given to them, <u>that they may be one even as we are one. I in them and you in me, that they may become perfectly one</u>, so that the world may know that you sent me and loved them even as you loved me." (17:22-23)

• "Father, I desire that they also, whom you have given me, may be with me where I am, to see my glory that you have given me before the foundation of the world." (17:24)[4]

It is absolutely vital that we understand what Jesus prayed here for the Early Church and for us. We are united with them through a faith that is *"built on the foundation of the apostles and prophets, Christ Jesus himself being the cornerstone, in whom the whole structure, <u>being joined together</u>, grows into a holy temple in the Lord." (Ephesians 2:20)*

So, let's humbly reflect on what Jesus prayed for us. He prayed that we would have an extraordinary unity. One likened to that existing between the Father and the Son! A unity that actually takes them into account, as

---

[4] We will examine this part of Christ's prayer in Appendix One – Christ's Glory Today

it literally involves them! A unity, He prayed, ***"that they also may be in us."*** Not merely "like us." But, "in us." An actual partnership with God! How many of us really see our fellowship with each other that deeply? Are we committed to one another in the same sense that we are committed to the Lord? That question should humble and melt us before the Lord! May we see as never before how we have been opposing the prayer of Jesus by our often inherited, selfish divisions and cool, unsympathetic distance from one another.

But there's much more! Somehow our unity is designed to prove something to unbelievers around us. I hope we can better see how incomplete the interpretations have been that affirm this prayer was totally fulfilled in the invisible, spiritual unity of the Universal Church. Many preachers and commentators have promoted that interpretation and, thereby, exonerated us from its fullest fulfillment. Have we embraced an interpretation that opposes His intended outcomes of world-wide astonishment and mass salvation? Have we laid aside a strategy because of the repentance and hard work it would take to return to it? I am afraid, perhaps, that it is so.

I respond to the easy and unfruitful interpretation by asking a simple question:

How much of the **spiritual** unity of the Church can the world **see**? Absolutely zero. The world does not see the spiritual. This prayer must refer to a visible, obvious unity. Instead of seeing our culture-crossing, paradigm-crushing, uniting love, the world sees us as hopelessly and stubbornly divided. And what is the outcome? Not salvation – but scoffing.

We will soon marvel at how the prayer of Jesus was initially fulfilled before the world's eyes in Jerusalem. But first, what does Jesus want our love and unity to reveal to the world? ***"…so that the world may believe that you sent me and loved them as you love me" (17:23).***

WHAT??? God loves us (and the world) like He loves Jesus? If we were able to understand this and believe it, we would view and treat one another (and them) very differently, wouldn't we? Yet, John 3:16 is the first verse most of us memorized. Remember how it starts? ***"For God so loved the world…."*** What is the word for love there? It is agape. The pure, perfect, deepest love conceivable – the love of God! Imagine, God loves us and unbelievers with the same kind of love that He has for His Son! John, in his first epistle, amplifies the ramifications of this truth. He repeatedly writes that we must love the world and one another with the same kind of love that we say that we have for God, Himself. See for yourself.[5]

Next, we can better understand why Jesus chose the sacred word, **"glory"** to express the nature of our unity as believers. It is a glorious and awesome thing. Powerful. Impacting. Radiant! It both warms everything while it also exposes the darkness around it. Truly, it is time to cry out in repentance, as I ask myself just how real and impactful is my love for my fellow-Christians? Not for a few in my own church. But for them all. Every one we meet is family. Forever! Part of my body, as we all compose the body of Christ. We know how it is suicidal to mistreat our bodies. Yet haven't many of us helped kill the power and purity of the Church by our refusal to love one another with the love of God?

Friends, we only get the **"well done"** by Jesus on that day IF we so love one another! Right?

"Lord, when did we see you hungry and feed you, or thirsty and give you a drink? And when did we see you a stranger and welcome you, or naked and clothe you? And when did we see you sick or in prison and visit you? And the King will answer

---

[5] See 1 John 2:7-11; 3:1; 3:11-18; 3:23-24; 4:7-21; 5:1-3

them, 'Truly, I say to you, as you did it to one of the least of these my brothers, you have done it to me.'" (Matthew 25:37-40)

All I can do now is to confess to Father and to you – I am so sorry. I have not loved either Jesus or you, my brothers and sisters, as I should. I have not sought His will or your good as I should. I have not cared for you as I ought. As Christ, my precious Lord, prayed that I would. God knows, as I write this – I am undone! No wonder the world thinks so poorly of us—and of Christ! We bear His Name. He gave us **His glory**. And what are we doing with it? Holy Spirit, help me! Help us all!

How much, if any, of this prayer of Jesus Christ for future believers was answered in the 1st century? How much of His prayer has been answered since New Testament times? And, is any of it being answered in our day, the 21st century?

It must deeply concern us, dear ones, if we find it not being answered in us and our churches today. He who was just about to be forsaken by His chosen Apostles, and soon thereafter to die for our sins – here, in John 17, <u>prayed for us</u>. How dare we receive the benefits of His atoning death without desiring to fulfill His will as it was expressed in this prayer uttered just before He died for us?

We have tried so many ways to reach the world for Christ. But there is one primary way that many of us have ignored: by loving one another openly and constantly with the love of God. We have forgotten that ***"Love never fails." (1 Corinthians 13:8)*** I now understand how I cannot honestly share the love of God with the world unless it is driving my relationships with other believers. We, ourselves, must first be transformed by love. Then, by His grace, we just might be powerfully used to lead others into this wonderful new life in Christ.

Chapter Three

The Prayer Answered in ACTS

What we would expect to happen after Jesus prayed, did happen. God began answering the prayer of Jesus in Jerusalem under the leadership of the Apostles. Read Acts 1 and pay close attention to the demand made by Jesus that they remain in Jerusalem until they receive the gift of the Holy Spirit (Acts 1:4-5). Because it was only through the empowerment of the Spirit that they could be the courageous, true and loving witnesses capable of fulfilling Christ's Great Commission. Power to proclaim Christ and live for Him, is an evidence that the Spirit has **"come upon you"** (1:8).

So, the Apostles waited. For ten days. Prayerfully. Welcoming other disciples, eventually totaling 120 (1:12-15). They, with prayer, waited on the Lord and He (Jesus-1:24) selected a replacement for the betrayer, Judas Iscariot (Acts 1:16-26). Matthias became the 12th Apostle. Christ, though having ascended to heaven, was present with His Church, just as He promised He would be. *"And behold, I am with you always, to the end of the age." (Matthew 28:20)*

Now, we always marvel as we read how these prayerful first disciples were baptized with the

Spirit while they were all assembled together (2:1). A mighty wind. Tongues of fire on their heads. Speaking languages they had never learned. The enactment of what Joel prophesied centuries before (Acts 2:16-21).

Peter, the fisherman-turned-Apostle preached a powerful message, not all of which is recorded (2:40). They begged him to tell them how to respond and turn to the Lord, whom they had crucified. He said,

"Repent and be baptized every one of you in the name of the Jesus Christ for the forgiveness of your sins, and you will receive the gift of the Holy Spirit. For the promise (of the Spirit) is for you and for your children and for all who are far off, everyone whom the Lord our God calls to himself" (2:38-39).

Those who received Peter's message by repentance and baptism were about 3,000 in number (2:41). After they received the gift of the Holy Spirit, how did they live? And how did it impact the world in Jerusalem?

The Disciples' Early UNITY

Remembering what Jesus prayed, consider how these first disciples were supernaturally **unified** as they waited and received the Holy Spirit.

• They all returned in obedience of Jesus' command to stay in Jerusalem (1:12)

• They stayed together in an Upper Room (1:13)

• They devoted themselves to praying together with others (1:14)

• Then they agreed on a process to choose Judas' replacement, by nominating two men and leaving the decision to the Lord. They all agreed that Matthias should replace Judas. Unity remained even in making a choice between two options. (1:24-26)

• The Apostles were all united in one place on the day of Pentecost (2:1)

• They were all filled with the Holy Spirit similarly and equally (2:2-3)

• They all spoke "the mighty works of God" in languages they did not know (2:4-11)

It is obvious that Luke was making the effort to depict the amazing unity of the Apostles throughout these ten remarkable days. As you reflect on the Lord's prayer in John 17, remember how He prayed that they would be **"one."** Remarkably unified. How remarkable was their unity? Luke summarizes[6] the unified

---

[6] Greek scholars note that the precise Greek form used by Luke in these verses is different from his normal way of describing the particular events throughout Acts. In this way, his readers realized

lifestyle of these early believers, in this, the first church, with the following astonishing words:

"And they devoted themselves to the apostles' teaching and the fellowship, to the breaking of bread and the prayers. And awe came upon every soul, and many wonders and signs were being done through the apostles. <u>And all who believed were together and had all things in common</u>. And they were selling their possessions and belongings and distributing the proceeds to all, as any had need. And day by day, attending the temple together and breaking bread in their homes, they received their food with glad and generous hearts, praising God and having favor with all the people. And the Lord added to their number day by day those who were being saved." (Acts 2:42-47)

I had never connected this remarkable lifestyle with the Lord's John 17 prayer. But it is an obvious answer to His prayer. They showed miraculous unity. They exhibited generous and selfless love to one another. Such a way of life

---

he was giving a progress report or general depiction of church life. Other summaries throughout Acts may be found in 4:32-35; 5:12-16; 6:7; 9:31; 12:24; 13:49; 16:5; 19:20 and 28:31.

that all who saw it were highly impressed by it. And what happened as a result? There were daily conversions! How many of the "outreach strategies" of our churches have shown any fruit like that? Most Evangelical churches in the USA have either plateaued or are in decline. But not them. In the midst of great external opposition and some internal hypocrisy, they continued unified and kept growing. Remember what Jesus taught the Apostles on that last night,

"A new commandment I give to you, that you love one another: just as I have loved you, you also are to love one another. <u>By this all people will know that you are my disciples, if you have love for one another."</u> *(John 13:34-35)*

They were showing what love looked like to the watching world. And the world was seeing the difference between their own lives and those transformed by the saving grace of God.

Right about now, while the tale has hardly been told, I think I have shared enough – and that you have read enough. That the same Spirit in us is saying the same thing to us all. We can do better. We must do better. That He, the blessed Holy Spirit, is ready to answer the prayer of Jesus in us. Out of love to Him, let's start desiring and praying for it. Then, soon, we will be driven with His agape love for the world. For,

"The Spirit and the Bride say, 'Come.' And let the one who hears say, 'Come.' And let the one who is thirsty come; let the one who desires take the water of life without price.'" (Revelation 22:17).

Chapter Four
The Jerusalem Church Unity

How long could it last? This life of united belief and behavior exhibited in the Early Church was truly miraculous. There are a few indicators in the Acts story of how much time[7] was lapsing between these early events. By the time we get to the second general summary (in 4:32-35), much had happened and the church had grown to around 5000 males. It was a very Jewish thing to count or emphasize men and not women. The actual number, including women and children, would have been many more. But happily, under the guidance of the Spirit, Luke was led to change his focus in the third progress report, and began counting women, too. And, the numbers were so great that he even stopped putting an exact number to the church (see 5:14)! But I am getting ahead of myself.

---

[7] According to Gene Edwards, they were probably well into the 4th year of existence. His very helpful <u>Revolutionary Bible Study</u> (2009) goes through every year from the crucifixion of Christ to the destruction of the Temple in 70 AD, showing what happened in Rome, in Jerusalem and in the Church each year.

Following the healing of a man crippled from birth (Acts 3:1-10) and another very powerful message by Peter (3:11-26), the devil tried to silence the church leaders by a gag order being issued from the very body which had plotted and promoted the crucifixion of Jesus, the Sanhedrim.

Perhaps a threat by this murderous Council would intimidate the Apostles enough to thwart Jesus' prayer from further fulfillment. So, they seized them and locked them up to sleep on the prospects of facing the fury of those who killed their Savior. Sorry Satan! When Peter answered them, he was still **"filled with the Holy Spirit" (4:8)** and he, with John, gave one of the most amazing defenses of faith ever written. (See 4:7-12). The Sanhedrim, **"when they saw the boldness of Peter and John and perceived that they were uneducated, common men, they were astonished ... seeing the man who was healed standing beside them, they had nothing to say in opposition." (4:13-14).**

The Jerusalem church had faced and overcome their first threat of violence from the government. They were learning, as John later would echo, the then-decades long proven truth:

"Little children, you are from God and have overcome them, for he who is in you is greater than he who is in the world." (1 John 4:4)

The Apostles went to their friends and reported what had just happened. Marvel at their unified response:

"And when they heard it, they lifted their voices together to God and said, 'Sovereign Lord … now look upon their threats and grant to your servants to continue to speak your word with all boldness, while you stretch out your hand to heal, and signs and wonders are performed through the name of your holy servant Jesus.' And when they had prayed, the place in which they were gathered together was shaken, and they were all filled with the Holy Spirit and continued to speak the word of God with boldness. (Acts 4:24-31)

The Disciples' Continued Unity

How long could this incredible way of life continue? Well, the answer is – as long as the Holy Spirit was in charge. As long as His grace and power were flowing. Remember the emphasis Jesus had made of waiting to go into the world until they were filled with the Spirit.

Now, let's see how Luke described the condition of the church at Jerusalem following this persecution and prayer.

"Now <u>the full number of those who believed were of one heart and soul,</u> and no one said that any of the things that belonged to him was his own, but <u>they had everything in common</u>. And with great power the apostles were giving their testimony to the resurrection of the Lord Jesus, and great grace was upon them all. There was not a needy person among them, for as many as were owners of lands or houses sold them and brought the proceeds of what was sold and laid it at the apostles' feet, and it was distributed to each as any had need." (Acts 4:32-35)

With every astonished glance that we take on these first- and second-generation disciples, we must remember that what we are seeing is the answer to Jesus' John 17 prayer. That the Father would bond in unity His children and use that to convict and draw the world to Jesus.

Luke portrays a remarkably united church, with few exceptions to this selfless way of life. We should understand that their dispossessing themselves to meet the needs of their fellow believers was highly unusual! For, many of these people were not family, close friends or acquaintances whom they were supporting.[8] They treated their new fellow-believers as family! And you can be sure, they did not have the disposable income that we in the West enjoy. They could not just go to the ATM and withdraw the cash that their fellow disciples needed. It was quite an ordeal for them to liquidate their property into cash. But they did it, gladly and generously.[9]

____

[8] Scholars estimate that during one of the three annual Pilgrim Feasts (like Pentecost), the population of Jerusalem would multiply 2 to 4 times. So, 50,000 normal residents could expand to between 100,000 and 200,000 Jewish inhabitants. That is why at least 15 different language groups are noted (see Acts 2:5-11) as being spoken by the Jews seeing and hearing Acts 2 unfold. When they were saved, many wanted to overstay their planned visit, far exceeding their budget. This created the immediate need for basic living support – which the believers were happy to supply, selling some of their extra houses and property and donating what they wanted to the church.

[9] Not everyone in Acts 4 sold every house or piece of property, as we see people owning their own homes following this (See 5:42; 8:3; 12:12, etc). The case of Barnabas is mentioned, at least so that

You can be certain that this widespread, Spirit-empowered exhibition of love for one another drew attention. It set off the Jerusalem church as a very different type of Jewish people. And their favor grew, spreading throughout Jerusalem and beyond. Just as Jesus had prayed. Which brings us to the church's next threat to its love and unity: Ananias and Sapphira.

Read the story for yourself (5:1-11). This husband and wife conspired to sell some property, agreeing not to give it all to the church. Rather, they pretended to give it all. And they were miraculously found out! Note these particulars:

• Peter declared that **"Satan had filled their hearts"** leading them to **"lie to the Holy Spirit." (5:3)**
• They had every right to give only a portion if they wanted to (5:4). But, they tried to deceive, pretending to be totally generous and not covetous.
• Peter announces, **"you have not lied to man but to God,"** (5:4) and Ananias drops dead (5:5), with Sapphira, 3 hours later,

---

all would be clear that this was not some demanded communalism (See 4:36-37).

following the same charade not knowing her husband had died. Before dropping dead herself, Peter asked a question, *"**How is it that you have agreed together to test the Holy Spirit of the Lord?"** (5:7-11)

It is no wonder that Luke describes the effect this had throughout the area with these words. ***And great fear came upon the whole church and upon all who heard of these things." (5:5b, 11)***
It was obvious that Peter, the other leaders, and the Lord wanted all to understand and believe this truth: that the Jerusalem church was directly united with the triune God: Father, Son and Spirit. And that we ought not mess with God! Especially regarding His glorious UNITY. The church's unity was a very sacred thing. Ananias and Sapphira, like Achan of old, (see Joshua 7:10-26), broke that unity through their greed and deception. They needed to have the lesson re-enforced: *our unity is to be constantly guarded and prized.* I pray that you will develop a flaming desire for this spirit to return to our churches today.
Did this so frighten the world that they kept their distance from the church, not wanting to be saved? We might reason so; but just the opposite happened. And, again, the John 17 prayer is answered. Here's Luke's next entry in describing the progress report following this breathtaking event:

"Now many signs and wonders were regularly done among the people by the hands of the apostles. And they were all together in Solomon's Portico. None of the rest dared join them, but the people held them in high esteem. And more than ever believers were added to the Lord, multitudes of both men and women, so that they even carried out the sick into the streets and laid them on cots and mats, that as Peter came by at least his shadow might fall on some of them. The people also gathered from the towns around Jerusalem, bringing the sick and those afflicted with unclean spirits, and they were all healed." (Acts 5:12-16)

So, here's the state of the church in Jerusalem after its first 5 years:

• The Spirit of unity continued to bond the believers together as they met in the large roofed area bordering the inside area of the Temple known as the Court of the Gentiles or the Outer Court.

• They did not make it an area for mass evangelism, but for worship and training. Non-believers feared to join those public gatherings. But they did not fear the personal contact with believers, which led to the greatest yet infusion of new believers being **"added to their number."**

• Instead of declining in any way, the power of God grows, with miracles of salvation, healing and deliverance at a **"more than ever"** rate!

• In fact, every sick and demonized person who came into Jerusalem and in contact with the Apostles, was healed. Note, the power was so flowing through them that contact with even a shadow could bring deliverance!

So, the unity and testimony of the Jerusalem church were often tested by the devil, yet it endured. United. Effective. Miracle-producing. Multiplying. Satan would then heighten his strategy to extinguish the church by eliminating its leaders through terrible persecution. Would he succeed and will we see the prayer of Jesus defeated? I think you know the answer.

Chapter Five
The Jerusalem Church Tested, Dispersed yet United

The book of Acts is evidence to how well Jesus made disciples. And to the absolute necessity of yielding to the control and guidance of the indwelling Holy Spirit in fulfilling His Great Commission globally.[10] But, it also reveals the many ways that the devil attempts to distract and divide us from following the Lord in the fullness of the Spirit.

In Acts 5 and 6, Satan stirs up opposition from outside and inside the church of Jerusalem. The first was frontal. (5:17-41) The second, subtle. (6:1-7). Both pernicious attempts were overcome, as we will see.

The Sanhedrim again arrested the apostles. But they were miraculously released by an angel in the middle of the night![11] When the leaders

---

[10] Read through Acts and note the 57 times that the Holy Spirit is highlighted in our only inspired history of the Early Church.

[11] You can read of a very similar event happening not long ago to Brother Yun, crippled with broken legs, at the Zhengzhou #1 Maximum Security Prison, in China's Henan Province. See **The Heavenly Man** (2002) chapter 22, pp 251-

commanded the Apostles to be brought in for trial and could not find them in the prison, their chains having been unlocked, they "**were greatly perplexed**." (5:24) I guess so! Then, in the midst of their growing chaos, "**Someone came and told them, 'Look! The men whom you put in prison are standing in the temple and teaching the people." (5:25).**

Following their recapture, if you want to call it that, for who was really in control? They were examined, beaten severely, again forbidden to speak in the name of Jesus, and released (5:27-40). Their bold and unified response to the Sanhedrim was, *"We must obey God rather than men." (5:29)* Their spirit upon being released and after a beating meant to shame and break them is depicted as: *"Then they left the presence of the council, rejoicing that they were counted worthy to suffer dishonor for the name." (5:41)* And their subsequent practice did not vary: *"And every day, in the temple, and from house to house, they did not cease teaching and preaching that the Christ is Jesus." (5:42)* So, who won, Jesus or Satan? Whose will was done? Whose prayer was answered?

---

262. You will find it hard to put that book down once you pick it up and start reading.

This is no fairy tale. These were men and women just like us. Concerned for their families, wanting to live in peace. Lovers of their own people and city. Respectful of their leaders. But, utterly changed inside-out by their relationship with the risen Christ and His gift of the empowering Holy Spirit. Do we really want the same for us and our nation today? We pray for revival and renewal. But are we willing to experience what often accompanies revival?

Acts 6 begins with the internal threat of overlooked, Greek-speaking widows. The Apostles could not be distracted from their devotion *"to prayer and to the ministry of the word." (6:4)* So, the office of deacon was created to ensure that no such division would happen. The people, themselves, were to elect *"seven men of good repute, full of the Spirit and of wisdom, whom we will appoint to this duty." (6:3)* One of the chosen men was *"Stephen, a man full of faith and of the Holy Spirit." (6:5)* The result of the deacons' ministry is given in Luke's 4th summary of Jerusalem church life:

"And the word of God continued to increase, and the number of disciples multiplied greatly in Jerusalem, and a great many of the priests became obedient to the faith." (6:7)

The devil was thwarted again. He could not divide the people of God, though he tried to use prejudice and tradition to do so. You see, unity is always being threatened. And the threats are not easily or immediately overcome. But, when Spirit-filled leaders lead and obedient disciples follow, even the gates of hell cannot prevail against the Church!

However, you likely know the end of this story as recorded in Acts 6:8-7:60). Stephen, *"full of grace and power, was doing great wonders and signs among the people. Then some … rose up and disputed with Stephen. But they could not withstand the wisdom and the Spirit with which he was speaking." (6:8-10)*

So, the enemies of Christ and His gospel resorted to the same old pattern. Spreading lies, they convinced the Sanhedrim to examine and condemn him. And Stephen, after his defense, *"full of the Holy Spirit" (7:56),* was cruelly murdered by being stoned to death.

Surely, this must divide the church. For, how could such a heavenly man (see 6:15; 7:55-57) be allowed to die such a death? But, even with this, the first case of martyrdom, unity prevailed in a most amazing way.

Luke records the amazing facts in these words:

"... And there arose on that day a great persecution against the church in Jerusalem, and they were all scattered throughout the regions of Judea and Samaria, except the apostles.... But Saul was ravaging the church, and entering house after house, he dragged off men and women and committed them to prison. Now those who were scattered went about preaching the word (literally, "evangelizing") – Acts 8:1-4

With these words, the focus on the Jerusalem church ends. The Church of Christ is about 7 years old. There no longer is a church freely and outwardly worshiping in Jerusalem. It has been decimated. The rest have been dispersed. What happens is the amazing, further answer to the prayer of our Lord in John 17 – His World-changing Prayer.

• Satan now plays his hand – divide and conquer - Cut off the head of the snake (the Apostles) and the snake will die
• Wrong! The Head is Christ Jesus the Lord, and the life flowed through the Spirit, not merely through the leadership!
• Jesus employs the persecution to send out the church, since they have been thoroughly discipled (see 6:1) and enabled now to make disciples outside of Jerusalem.

- The last progress report stated, ***"the number of disciples multiplied greatly" (6:7)***

At first, converts were added daily (2:47), then multitudes were added to their number (5:14), then the disciples were increasing (6:1), and finally, the disciples multiplied greatly (6:7). Luke does not use precise mathematical terms. But what we see here is addition becoming multiplication. Regular conversion growth becoming the exponential growth of the discipleship prayed for by Jesus and demanded by His Great Commission! Disciples MULTIPLY because each disciple is trained with the expectation of reproduction.[12]

Having worked through the issue of prejudice within Judaism, the disciples are now ready to learn how to reach the wider world. But they do it incrementally, first to Judeans, then to Samarians, then to Antiochans and then globally. Remember the map of King Jesus as revealed in Acts 1:8?

"But you will receive power when the Holy Spirit has come upon you, and you will be

---

[12] We carefully explain this in the books *Are you a Christian or a Disciple? (2014) and Disciple the Nations! (2023)*

Prejudice and greed are hard to overcome. And how can you love one another in true unity if prejudice and selfishness are active? You cannot. So, until the leaders led the Church into indiscriminate love for everyone, just as God loves the world, the Church would not know how to love Gentiles as part of God's family. Acts shows this progress in chapters 10-15.[13]

With you, I read the book of Acts and wonder – do I really fit in? Sure, I claim that I believe it and assure others of its divine inspiration. But what has happened? We are so divided today in Christianity. Even among born again, Spirit-filled, Bible-believing Christians, there is almost no unity as we have seen depicted in the Early Church.

I will address the reality of our division, loss of spiritual power and divine love in the second section. But, right now, after what we have read, we should be feeling a bit uneasy. Convicted. Even shaken. Where is the glory in

---

[13] Until it became official that Gentiles could be discipled and embraced equally, the scattered church apparently only discipled Jews – Acts 11:1-19

the Church today? Where is the love of believers for one another producing a great wonder from the world? And an attraction to this Jesus, who is the Center of it all? Where are the miracles which affirmed God's approval from heaven? To me, it simply does not look like the prayer of Jesus is being answered today in our lives and churches in the West. Does it to you?

Is the lack of all this simply because His prayer has been already answered, and His will already fulfilled? Some would argue, theologically, that such is the case. The time of miracles, healings, mass conversions are past. We are the remnant and should not expect them today.

Well, I will show you where it is happening today. And this will prove wrong the theology denying Christ's prayer is still intact, ready to be fulfilled. And in a greater way than ever yet seen. I want you to see and believe that it can happen today. That the World-changing Prayer of Jesus is still being amazingly answered today. Then you will have to decide for yourselves whether you want it fulfilled in and through you – or not.

PART TWO

The Warning of Jesus to Us Today

Chapter Six
The Wisest Way Forward

We cannot overlook the obvious. Christianity is in an incredibly divided condition. And that glaring problem is a huge impediment to our witness to the world. Many non-Christians have noted our lack of love and collegiality, and it has turned them off. What must the God, who is love (1 John 4:8), be thinking?

His eternal and beloved Son prayed for our unity. A unity that would be glorious -- attracting and discipling unbelievers by the millions. And we have seen what happened in Acts and the Early Church as a result. Multitudes were saved by beholding the love of believers for each other and for them. They saw the sacrifice they were willing to bear just to deliver Christ and His Gospel to them. Jesus' prayer had a wonderful first stage answer then. But what about today? Do we love one another? What about the countless divisions that we are cherishing rather than each other?

Just think of them. We have:

• Christian Protestants vs. Christian Catholics vs. Christian Orthodox
• Traditional vs. Contemporary Christians
• Calvinistic vs. Arminian Christians

- Reformed vs. Dispensational Christians
- Charismatic vs. Non-Charismatic Christians
- Trichotomists vs. Dichotomists
- Premill vs. Amill vs. Postmill vs. Panmill Christians
- Pretrib vs. Midtrib vs. Posttrib
- Denominational vs. Independent Christians
- KJV only vs. other Bible Translation Christians
- Anglican vs. Baptist vs. Church of Christ vs. Episcopal vs. Lutheran vs. Mennonite vs. Messianic Jewish vs. Methodist vs. Nazarene vs. Pentecostal vs. Presbyterian vs. Wesleyan Christians – with each of them further divided within themselves into scores of splinter groups

And in the local churches there are countless divisions between ordained and laity, educated and uneducated, rich and poor, male and female, White and Black and Asian and Hispanic, old and young, singing and silent, kneeling and sitting, hands raised and hands in pockets – the list is almost endless. Looking at today's Christian reality, one might think that the one thing Christians must agree on is – **we must be divided!** Whose will is being accomplished in our divisions? Not the will of the One who prayed in John 17. Not the will of Christ the Lord.[14]

How can we deal with this huge problem? Is there anything we can do or is there too much water over the dam? Is the Church irrevocably divided? Can we make a difference against this strong current that seems to be sweeping us all away? C. S. Lewis might help us here:

"We all want progress. But progress means getting nearer to the place where you want to be. And if you have taken a wrong turning, then to go forward does not get you any nearer. If you are on the wrong road, progress means doing an about-turn and walking back to the right road; and in that case the man who turns back soonest is the most progressive."[15]

I have decided to devote only one chapter to our division, knowing it will seem ridiculously simplistic and naïve to many. But I am willing to appear that way, because I truly think it is the wisest way forward.

Please, hear me clearly - I am not advocating that we scrap our convictions. Rather, that we must realize this: *not every truth is of equal value.*

---

[14] For further discussion see Appendix Two – Are the Divisions Worth it?
[15] In CS Lewis, *Mere Christianity*, p. 36

That not every belief is worth dividing over.[16] This, I think, is the wisest way to unite and move forward. I do not seek absolute doctrinal unity, or worship unity, or confessional unity, or cultural unity, or denominational unity, or …. Rather, I seek and pray for missional unity. Kingdom unity. We do not need Uniformity but Unity. You might be in serious disagreement with me. But …

Are you ready for a shock? What I now propose is something you should seriously consider and pray about implementing. Every one of you. Immediately. How can I be so sure? Because I know that what I am now asking you to do is the will of God! Revealed in His Word. By the ascended and reigning Lord. I saw this for the first time last week as I was praying and meditating on the Word.

The revelation was delivered to a great church in the 1st century. A church that was busy but in serious decline. What you will read in the next few pages is what Jesus wants you to do. In fact, He warns us that if we do not change, it may result in His opposing and removing our

---

[16] For those thinking that we can only go forward by believing the same truths, debating and defending them, and demanding that we all reach the same biblical conclusions -please read Appendix Two – Are the Divisions Worth It?

church and ministry. Just read below what He demanded of one of the greatest churches of the 1ˢᵗ century – the church at Ephesus:

"I know your works, your toil and your patient endurance, and how you cannot bear with those who are evil, but have tested those who call themselves apostles and are not, and found them to be false. I know you are enduring patiently and bearing up for my name's sake, and you have not grown weary.

"But I have this against you, that you have abandoned the love you had at first. Remember therefore from where you have fallen; repent, and do the works you did at first. If not, I will come to you and remove your lampstand[17] from its place, unless you repent." (Revelation 2:2-5)

May we all understand the implications of these clear and ominous words:

• Our Christian lives and ministries (our "works") may be both extensive and sacrificial

---

[17] The lampstand was a reference to their church – see Rev 1:20. This was a promise by Jesus – He would remove their church if they did not remember, repent and return to their first love!

("toil"), yet we still be opposed by Christ the Head, and our church be lost.

• We might fight to retain our church's theological purity through statements of orthodoxy, church discipline, and lose in the end. Our determination to define and defend the truth (a great strength), can become a distraction (our greatest weakness).

• We might "patiently endure" Christian opposition and persecution for the sake of Jesus, even giving thanks for suffering "for His name's sake," and still, terminally, dishonor Him.

What was Jesus really saying to the Ephesians and to us? He is not saying that truth doesn't matter. All of the good things He listed, that the Ephesians were committed to, were biblical. They were right. But, make no mistake about this. Jesus Christ our King is here warning an historic and famous church[18] that ***Love matters most to Him!*** That is the revelation we must grasp if our missional unity is to conquer our crippling divisions.

The Spirit-filled agape love of devotion that they first had - for Him, for their fellow believers, and for the lost world around them -

---

[18] This church was founded and pastored by Paul, and led, later by both Timothy and the Apostle John!

is what He declared that the Ephesian church had lost. They had allowed many good things to replace the one, indispensable thing. And so have many of us. I know this first hand, because it happened to me. After I returned from the mission field and was called to pastor a church in Philadelphia, PA. I have told the painful story elsewhere.[19] I had to be pruned, to be chastened by the Lord, in order to bear more fruit (see John 15:2; Hebrews 12:5-11).

So, what did I do? I did not scrap either my Reformed theology or denomination. But I did what Jesus told all of us to do if we find ourselves lacking in 1 Corinthians 13 love. It is right there in the Word. Three clear and difficult things: *remember, repent and return*. This, briefly, is what Jesus is demanding of a church (and Christians) who have lost their love. We cannot display John 17 unity without 1 Corinthians 13 love.

Remember

Jesus wants me to remember what I was before He saved me. The life of sin that I was living. The mess I and my family were in. Together with the hopelessness and despair that filled my soul. And He wants me to remember the

---

[19] ***Let Love Win through YOU*** (reprinted – 2023 by Parson's Porch Book).

change that happened when He was enthroned in my life. The immediate joy! The gratitude and praises to God that flowed from my lips. The tears from my eyes. The love that consumed me. The desire I had for His Word and His people. For Him.

He also wants me to remember the immediate concern that filled my heart for my family and friends who had not yet been born again by faith in Him. How I had to tell them what had happened to me. And to share the simple truths of the Gospel with them – imploring them to receive Jesus as their Lord and Savior.

Paul, knowing how love may be lost, reminded the Colossians of the best way to retain it, in these words: *"**Therefore as you received Christ Jesus the Lord, so walk in him....**"* *(**Colossians 2:6**).* Unfortunately, many of us have moved on from Christ, the Uniter. We have moved on, to many other priorities and principles and projects – and left our initial love. "The honeymoon is over."

Jesus wants us to remember what the Holy Spirit told Jeremiah to *"**go and proclaim in the hearing of Jerusalem**"*:

*"**Thus says the Lord, I remember the devotion of your youth, your love as a bride, how you followed me in the wilderness, in**"*

a land not sown. Israel was holy to the Lord, the first fruits of his harvest...." (*Jeremiah 2:2-3*)

It is good to remember what God remembers, for we are the children of God. It is good to start each day filled with love for God and humankind.

Why does Jesus command us, first, to **remember** these things? Because they were the best of days. High and holy days. Glorious in their simplicity and in their peace. Days that came at great cost to Him. Days for us that arose with the sun shining, because He endured on the day when the sun refused to shine. How long has it been since we lovingly remembered Him and rededicated ourselves to Him?

He commands us, *"**Remember therefore from where you have fallen...."** (Rev 2:8)* When we forget those early days of faith and love, we fall. When we begin our days without joy and surrender – we fall. When we start to forget what He saved us from, and the spirit of humility it produces, we grow proud and – we fall.

Paul was filled with the same Spirit that filled Jesus. So, he said virtually the same thing to the Galatians that Jesus said to the Ephesians:

"O foolish Galatians! Who has bewitched you? ...Let me ask you only this: Did you receive the Spirit by works... or by hearing with faith? Are you so foolish? Having begun by the Spirit, are you now being perfected by the flesh?" (Galatians 3:1-3)

He summarized their condition in this way, *"you have fallen from grace" (5:4-NKJV).* Like the Ephesians, they had fallen. They had forgotten grace and embraced works. And grace is a special New Testament word. Grace is <u>God's love to the undeserving.</u> Grace, then, is a special kind of love, a **super love**. It is the first word of greeting and last word of benediction written in many of the letters of Christ's Apostles. The Spirit who inspired their letters wanted all New Testament believers, and us, to be love-driven. To never fall from God's super agape – His grace.

Paul was right. The Galatians were foolish to forget the super love of God that had saved them. Jesus, when exalted at the right hand of God and sending a message to the Ephesian Christians, commanded them to remember how they started. When was the last time you remembered those wonderful, early days of faith, when you sang:

"Jesus is all the world to me, my life, my joy - my all"

<u>**Repent**</u>

Repentance is a natural next step to those who remember how greatly we have fallen. We know that to repent is to do a complete turn – 180 degrees. It is a total change of mind. It is not an emotion, though it often produces great emotion. Today, it usually refers to what unbelievers must do to be saved. But it is rarely a word spoken to Christians. To the saved. We often see ourselves as those who have repented. Not as those who need to repent.

But Jesus used this word when speaking to a famous Christian church. In fact, five out of seven of those churches to whom He sent letters in Revelation 2-3, were commanded to repent.[20] Christians need to repent when we replace what is primary with what is secondary. When we leave our first love. Or bury it under 100 other good-but-insufficient strategies.

Friends, love is the first or greatest commandment, according to Jesus. All the Law and the Prophets depend on it or hang beautifully from it. (See Matthew 22:34-40) Without God's agape love, see what happens:

- to the tongues-speaker and prophet,

---

[20] See Rev 2:5; 2:16; 2:21-22; 3:3; 3:19

-     to the prayer warrior whose faith can remove mountains,
-     to lavish Christian givers who give away everything that they own,
-     even to the martyr who dies!

Paul writes, that all such wonderful people, without love, are ***"nothing"*** and will ***"gain nothing." (1 Corinthians 13:1-3)***

Did you hear that? Does it register? Our Lord will not accept or reward as truly Christian anything that leaves agape-love out! As such, He is declaring, all these "good works" without love are really "ungodly works." That is why we must repent whenever we forsake the way of godly love. Especially true is this of those co-workers with Christ now carrying His Gospel to the world.

I am asking you right now, to bow your heart and repent of leaving your first love – Jesus. Admitting to our Father what has taken His place in your life. What has rendered you practically powerless in living for one another – and for the lost. These are lovely Christian idols which we have erected. Which John, the aged Apostle of love, closed his letter reminding us of: ***"Little children, keep yourselves from idols." (1 John 5:21).*** Humbly express your sorrow. Come clean. Because you can.

"If we (believers) confess our sins, he is faithful and just to forgive us our sins and to cleanse us from all unrighteousness." (1 John 1:9)

It's time to repent before reading another word. Close the booklet. Cry out to our Father right now. Prodigal sons and daughters – let's come home.

Return

There is tremendous grace in the call to return! We may have left our first love BUT we have not lost it! Its weak embers can be rekindled. The wisest way forward is to step back from what we are doing and begin following Jesus in love – again. In the simple, New Testament way through which He guided and empowered the Early Church.

PART THREE

*The Prayer of Jesus
Answered TODAY*

Chapter Seven

Our Return to the Faith of the First Disciples

We have all prayed for <u>re</u>vival or <u>re</u>newal or <u>re</u>formation. These words have this in common – they begin with the letters "<u>re,</u>" signifying a return to something once known but left. We cannot experience any of these wonderful awakenings without stopping and going back. Our repentance is the first step of returning. We have stopped and turned. Now, by faith, we must take the next steps of returning.

Returning to Christ's message to the Ephesians, this should follow our repentance. The Lord commanded them, after they repent:

"…and do the works you did at first."
(Revelation 2:5)

This is far simpler than you think. So, do not overthink it. Just do it.

Let's agree on what all disciples of Jesus can agree on at the start. Let's take these baby steps. Think of it like we are planting a simple, single church – a real church of Christ – in your house. It will be composed of a repentant people, freshly liberated from sin, devoting themselves to fulfilling the John 17 Prayer of Jesus and, thereby, the Great Commission. In that order. Love for God and one another followed by love for the world. John 17 came before Jesus said, ***"Peace be with you. As the Father has sent me, even so I am sending you." (John 20:21)***

The call of Jesus follows that order: ***"Follow me and I will make you become fishers of men." (Mark 1:17).*** First, follow Christ yourself, and then make others to be disciples, helping them be and do what you are. The Great Commission is entailed in the original call; but it isn't given until the end – in Mark 16. We must be a disciple among disciples before we can make disciples of others. Or put another way, we cannot give away what we do not possess. We have saving faith at the outset; but Jesus did not say, "Go and make believers." He said,

"All authority in heaven and on earth has been given to me. Go therefore and make disciples of all nations…." (Matthew 28:18-19)

So, following our repentance, and, as we return to our first love, what are the few things we should do immediately? It is not as difficult a question as we might think. The difficulty comes in what might need to be relinquished or re-prioritized in our lives. Our goal is to find what is basic. And, please understand, I am not saying that where we agree to start is where we should remain. In fact, we must all grow beyond what I recommend. I will be suggesting a few foundational things, like the author of Hebrews did in 6:1-2. And, being foundational, just remember, they are to be practiced daily. The moment they are not done, the building process will become risky, because we have started building off-center. Not straight up. And it will not take much time before the whole structure begins to sway and, inevitably collapse.

The First Message of Peter

I start here because this is where the first church in Jerusalem started. After preaching a tremendous message (Acts 2:14-36), his hearers, **"cut to the heart,"** asked the Apostles, **"What shall we do?" (2:37).** Peter's answer provides the foundation that we should all agree on. So, let's start there. How did Peter answer their heart cries?

"And Peter said to them, 'Repent and be baptized every one of you in the name of Jesus Christ and you will receive the gift of the Holy Spirit.'" (2:38)

It would do us all well to take inventory of whether this foundation has been laid in our lives. The triple-layered foundation of Repentance, Jesus-centered water baptism and the baptism with the Holy Spirit.

Now, please recall that these early disciples did not have a Bible in their possession, like we do. Nor did they have a permanent building that was devoted to their times of worship and instruction. Also, the leaders were not proceeding in a way that demanded paying them a salary. Quite simply, we might say that they began with: No Bible, No Building and No Budget. Even though those three things seem indispensable to many of us. How would we survive as Christ-followers today without these wonderful things? Yet, they not only survived, as we have seen, they thrived and multiplied.

I see Peter's Spirit-empowered message, at its core, teaching the following fundamentals:

• **Repentance** of sin is a non-negotiable beginning for a believer
•The great sin Peter spoke of was rejection of Jesus as the Messiah of God and crying out for His death.
•Implied in this, was their rejection of the words Jesus taught as being the truth of God.

• **Baptism** of those who repent is to quickly follow. We know that baptism signifies the believer's union in Christ's death on the cross and His resurrection from the dead (See Romans 6:1-14). This baptism is a confession of faith and a pledge to walk in newness of life and not to live in sin any longer.[21]

• **Reception** of the promised Holy Spirit was linked with their water baptism. Note, that the Spirit is to be actively received, not to be passively presumed as part of the salvation process. I know there is disagreement concerning this baptism with the Spirit, and I have had to work through those issues. But this being more a booklet than a book, I will stop there and trust the Spirit to be your Teacher, just as He has been mine.[22]

---

[21] The explanation of a faith union with Christ would have preceded the baptism and been part of the "many other words" Peter spoke prior to their baptism, according to Acts 2:40. They would not have performed a baptism without the people knowing what they were confessing by submitting themselves to it.

[22] Please note what Peter promised in His message. That believers who were water baptized would *receive* Spirit baptism. Just as we *receive* Jesus (John 1:12), we are to *receive* the empowering Holy Spirit (Luke 11:13; John 7:38-39; Acts 19:1-7; Ephesians 5:18). So, in his statement to the

As we think of the Early Church's unity being a model for our own, let us reaffirm our (1) repentance, (2) confession of faith as formally declared at baptism, and (3) our need of the empowering presence of the Holy Spirit. This will produce in us the same foundation that led to the remarkable life of love and witness seen in the Jerusalem church.

For many years, my life and ministry did not strongly include the person and work of the Spirit. I followed my theological tradition in that way. But I have found that we cannot be united in love if we do not have the Spirit at work in us, for love is the fruit of the Spirit! (Galatians 5:22) Nor can we learn the Word

---

Sanhedrim, Peter argued that they could not stop preaching in Christ's name because God had made them His witnesses. **"And we are witnesses to these things, and so is the Holy Spirit, whom God has given to those who obey him." (Acts 5:32)** The Spirit is given following what obedience? I think, in context, he is referring to those who obeyed in repenting and being water baptized. This helps explain why Paul mentions believers' "one baptism" (Ephesians 4:5) when there are various baptisms (Hebrews 6:2) – water and Spirit baptism are to be seen and received in a connected way. The critical point, to me, is that water and Spirit baptism are linked.

rightly apart from the Spirit being our Teacher, according to Jesus (John 14:26), Paul (1 Corinthians 2:9-14) and John (1 John 2:20,27).

The disciples described in Acts, embodied supernatural love for each other and for the world, and became direct answers to the World-changing Prayer of Jesus. So, dear friends, let us join with them, remembering Peter's original message as it helps us return to the roots of ***"our common salvation." (Jude 3)*** From this foundation, we can proceed filled with His love for one another and the world.

Chapter Eight
Living in Divine Unity, TODAY

We agree that the Bible reveals that Christ's Kingdom, ultimately, will be composed of *"every tribe and language and people and nation." (Revelation 5:9)* Instead of focusing on our differences, I am asking you to focus more on our Head, Jesus. And what He prayed for and how we might get the job done more quickly than we could imagine. In this regard, our relationship with the Spirit, the Author of love in us, might have a more basic Great Commission connection and outcome than many of us have thought. This was Paul's focus, when he wrote to and prayed for His model church plant, those who, in fact had reached their region for Christ (See 1 Thessalonians 1:2-8; 3:12; 4:9-10).[23]

I believe that, largely, Disciple Making Movements (DMMs) are succeeding globally just because the emerging house churches are fulfilling the John 17 Prayer of Jesus! It has

---

[23] I examine the love-based strategy and success of the Thessalonians in *The Amazing Love of Paul's Model Church: How the Thessalonians became disciples and reached their region with the Gospel.*

been shown, and is increasingly being written, how Muslims, Hindus, Buddhists, Communists, Animists and Atheists are all being captivated by the love of today's DMM-producing disciples! This is happening globally. The world is being convinced by the love these disciples have for each other – and for them! I am seeing it in Pakistan and Africa, just as missionaries are wherever they are ministering.

The shocking reality is that of the roughly 2000 DMMs being carefully tracked globally, only around 30 have emerged in the USA! And those few are arising, not so much through established Evangelical churches, but, rather through immigrant communities and prisons! Could it be that our refusal to live by the love of the Spirit, generously and freely, is a canceling sin in the churches of the largely materialistic Western world? That DMMs cannot arise by the power of the Spirit until we remember, repent and return, ourselves?

And, please, endure me further. It is a fact that neither Pentecostal nor Charismatic churches in the USA are having more success in planting DMMs here than are non-Charismatic churches! So, a church's being familiar with the things of the Spirit does not always qualify one to take part in today's great spiritual renewals. Perhaps less focus on tongues/prophecy and more focus on the more excellent way of love would help here, just as it did in Corinth.[24]

I will at the end of this booklet share a list of 15 suggestions that, in my opinion, might help ignite among us, a return to an Acts-like life of love that has supernatural, missional, multiplying power.[25] But, first, I will recommend three things for the LCWE delegates in Seoul and for all of us, globally:

(1) Take what you hear and experience at Lausanne IV (and after) seriously and personally – every day going forward. God is

---

[24] I have been greatly helped by Dr. RT Kendall's and Dr. Michael Brown's writings on the Spirit. Kendall refers to himself as a Reformed charismatic (Big R little c – his emphasis). He was the chosen successor of Dr Martyn Lloyd Jones, the famous Reformed pastor/author who often defended the post conversion baptism with the Holy Spirit. Dr. Kendall believes that the emphasis on tongues in today's Charismatic/Pentecostal churches is a major cause for division among Bible believing Christians. He writes much to help clarify this issue and bring together "the Word" and "the Spirit sides" of the Church. Dr. Brown has often done the same, carefully analyzing and critiquing Charismatic excesses to help bridge the gap between these factions in the Church.
[25] See Appendix Three – Time to Start Afresh

bringing you TOGETHER with others for such a time as this. Let the meetings He places you in change your lives.

(2) Take time listening to those you meet (or read of) who come from the non-Western countries in which DMMs are flourishing. Listen and take notes, because the Holy Spirit is saying YES to them and to their simple, prayer-driven, love-empowered ministries. They are poised to show us the way forward. They will help us answer Jesus' Prayer, just as they are most remarkably doing.

(3) Ask the Lord how you (like me) from the West can come alongside of our non-Western brothers and sisters in financial assistance. You see, that was a key component of the Acts 2-5 fulfillments of Jesus' Prayer. Many Western Christians have much more available capital and can reach out advocating for the needs of our non-Western fellow disciples. It has been one of the greatest joys of my life to leverage my influence in this way in their behalf.[26]

I must finish this short book, to get it to my publisher before our trip to Africa. So, please

---

[26] A careful study and application of Luke 11:5-10 will show that Jesus has promised advocates effectiveness in fundraising for other's needs, rather than asking for themselves. This would revolutionize missions and missionary support raising if understood and practiced – in the Spirit.

consider these words so imperfectly and briefly shared with you. May it birth in many of you a paradigm shift in strategy. And may it also stimulate more amicable debate and discussion in refining how we can unite to fulfill both the Prayer and Great Commission of our Lord Jesus. In humbling ourselves, let us join Paul's strategy *"to become all things to all people, that by all means (we) might save some." (1 Corinthians 9:22)* And thus, I believe we can return to the place of greatest missional blessing, and be an answer to the World-changing Prayer of Jesus.

I pray that we will unite in believing that, even now in Seoul, South Africa, Sao Paolo, and San Francisco, indeed globally, it is still true that,

"The eyes of the Lord run to and fro throughout the whole earth to give strong support to those whose heart is whole toward him" (2 Chronicles 16:9)?

Whatever has divided us outwardly, has developed from our having a divided heart. May God help each of us remove those divisions, wherever possible, within the limits of our biblically-informed consciences. Start today, right where you are. How can we expect His *"strong support"* and help if we ignore the heart cry of His Son in John 17?

In closing, there are some who will think that my effort in this message is simplistic, sinister or worse. Some will misread it as a love vs. truth approach (which it isn't). It is, rather, a call to **"speak the truth in love."** (Eph 4:15), which Paul urges at the close of his powerful words promoting the unity of the Spirit. I believe that there is a way **"to contend for the faith" (Jude 3)**, without dividing true disciples of Christ. With you, I deeply love Christ and His Church. So, be sure, I am not asking for you to compromise. Just to prioritize the Great Commission and Prayer of Jesus with devotion to the missional unity that existed in the New Testament Church. With you, I am willing to change to become an answer to our Lord's World-changing Prayer, which flowed from His spirit of overwhelming love for the world, **"not wishing that any should perish, but that all should reach repentance." (2 Peter 3:9)** May God bless and help us all reach the world in our generation.

*****

I am your brother and servant for the glory of Jesus and the fulfilling of His Great Commission by the power of His Spirit. If I can help you, come alongside of you, encourage, pray, or join with you in fulfilling the Great Commission, and for that which Jesus prayed, please contact me, understanding that I will ask for no financial remuneration for any service rendered:

Edward N Gross (Ed)Delaware, USA

Emails – ed.gross@comcast.net

edgross54@gmail.com

Cellphone (WhatsApp) (1) 215-805-2153

Appendix One
The Glory of Jesus Today

"Father, I desire that they also, whom you have given me, may be with me where I am, to see my glory that you have given me before the foundation of the world." (17:24)

This petition of Jesus is often interpreted as His desire that we would go to heaven when we die. But I join the many who believe that He was requesting something far more present and powerful than our ultimate realization in heaven.

Jesus was praying for the blessing of union with Him – NOW. This is undoubtedly the way that the Apostles understood it and realized it. Stephen, when he was martyred, ***saw the glory of God and Jesus standing at the right hand of God." (Acts 7:55)*** The Apostles and their disciples lived by faith in union with the risen Lord. What they did "in His name," they did in union with His ascended and reigning glory. The glorified Jesus was with them, ***"always, to the end of the age."*** (Matthew 28:20). He conferred on them the faith, love and gifts they would need by the filling of the Holy Spirit. The Spirit enabled them, by faith, to live powerfully "in Christ" rather than "in the world." In other words, they were not bound in their lives to their five senses. They *"reigned (as kings) in life through the one man Jesus Christ." (Romans 5:17)* They thanked God, *"who in Christ always leads us in triumphal procession, and through us spreads the fragrance of the knowledge of him everywhere." (2 Corinthians 2:14)*

This was no hyperbole. Their union was actual by faith, so, real power flowed through them in Jesus' name. And they expected the same to occur in the churches they planted and down through the ages. This is why they wrote to encourage them and us with these words:

• *"Blessed be the God and Father of our Lord Jesus Christ, who has blessed us in Christ with every spiritual blessing in the heavenly places" (Ephesians 1:3)*

• *"…If God be for us, who can be against us? He who did not spare his own Son but gave him up for us all, how will he not also with him graciously give us all things?" (Romans 8:31-32)*

• *"If then you have been raised with Christ, seek the things that are above, where Christ is, seated at the right hand of God. Set your minds on things that are above, not on things that are on the earth. For you have died and your life is hidden with Christ, in God." (Colossians 3:1-3)*

- *"Submit yourselves therefore to God. Resist the devil, and he will flee from you. Draw near to God, and he will draw near to you." (James 4:7-8)*
- *"His divine power has granted to us all things that pertain to life and godliness, through the knowledge of him who called us to his own glory and excellence, by which he has granted to us his precious and very great promises, so that through them you may become partakers of the divine nature, having escaped from the corruption that is in the world...." (2 Peter 1:3-4)*
- *"See what kind of love the Father has given to us, that we should be called the children of God; and so, we are." (1 John 3:1)*

"And so, we are!" These verses were not only for them. They are in the Bible because they are to be our experience, too. Many, since the Apostles' times, have so lived. And, how mightily God has used them! We, ourselves, are learning that the blessings of God are for now. What Paul said to the Corinthians, is true of us, *"...whether the world or life or death or the present or the future—<u>all are yours,</u> and you are Christ's, and Christ is God's." (1 Cor. 3:22).*

The prayer request of Jesus expresses His desire for us to be able to unite with Him, as He exists in His glory now. As the resurrected and reigning Lord. This can only be done by the work of the Holy Spirit, the author of our rebirth and first faith-Giver. It is by the Spirit that we can *abide in Christ.* How we can be with Him and be directed and empowered by Him. We are commanded to *"walk in the Spirit" or to "keep in step with the Spirit." (Gal. 5:16,25)* When we do, it must be through His Word, because the sword of the Spirit is the Word of God (Eph 6:17). What will the Spirit communicate to our spirits? *"He will guide you into all truth, for he will not speak on his own authority…He will glorify me, for he will take what is mine and declare it to you." (John 16:13-14)* So, it is the Holy Spirit's job to reveal to us the glory, power and promises of Christ. And we are to live by them. This is what it means to live "in Christ."

Our lives should be glorious, radiant. We are the light of the world, and commanded to let our light shine before others so that they may see our good works and give glory to God (Matt. 5:14-16) The glory of the love and truth of God, emanating from us, should draw many around us to Jesus. This can happen daily, if we are led and empowered by the Spirit of life and have the victory depicted in Romans 8:1-17.

Our power in life over sin and in prayer over all opponents of Christ, flows from understanding who we NOW are in Christ. I would suggest reading the works of Watchman Nee (like his Normal Christian Life), and of Andrew Murray (like his Abiding in Christ), for clear Bible teaching concerning our victory in Christ. I would recommend the biographies about the following men and women, together with their writings, to you. This will make you very excited about the great things that can be done today, in the name of Christ. I always read the life stories of people before I read their writings, if possible. These people have seen and walked in the glory of the risen Lord Jesus Christ![27] I have a manuscript of brilliant quotes from them and many others that I will send you for **<u>FREE</u>** by just emailing me and saying, "Send the Quotes!" (send to: ed.gross@comcast.net)

May God bless you, as you are strengthened to abide in Christ and make disciples globally! What Paul prayed for, all these great faith warriors have claimed, and you can, too: ***"Now***

---

[27] AJ Gordon, Andrew Murray, AB Simpson, William Seymour, John G Lake, Watchman Nee, Rees Howells, Jessie Penn Lewis, Samuel Howells, Martin Lloyd Jones, Smith Wigglesworth, Lester Sumrall, Juan Carlos Ortiz, Michael Brown, RT Kendall, Jim Cymbala

*to him who is able to do far more
abundantly than all we ask or think,
according to the power at work within us,
to him be glory in the church and in Christ
Jesus throughout all generations, forever
and ever. Amen." (Eph 3:20)*

Appendix Two

Are the Divisions Worth it?

Both Jesus and Paul clearly taught that not all truth is worth dividing over. And that perfect agreement or uniformity of belief among all His followers is not essential. In fact, they held back certain truths from some of their disciples because they were not yet ready to hear it, while sharing that truth with others who were ready.[28] So, let us do the same here, and trust God with the results. Paul put it like this:

"…But whatever gain I had, I counted as loss for the sake of Christ. Indeed, I count everything loss because of the surpassing worth of knowing Christ Jesus my Lord….and the power of his resurrection…. Brothers, I do not consider that I have made it my own. But one thing I do: forgetting what lies behind and straining forward to what lies ahead… I press on for … the upward call of God in Christ Jesus." (Philippians 3:7-14).

---

[28] See, for instance, Luke 6:41-42; 9:49-55; John 16:4, 12; Acts 1:7; 10:1-48; Rom. 14:1-23; 16:17; 1 Cor. 3:1-4; Heb 5:11-6:3; 1 Pet 4:8; 2 Pet 3:15-16; Rev. 2:24

Paul wanted the Philippians to leave the past and move forward. I think that is the wisest way for us, too. In fact, Paul's very next words were:

"Let those of us who are mature think this way, and if in anything you think otherwise, God will reveal that also to you. Only let us hold true to what we have attained." (3:15-16)

Let us grow up and move forward for Christ's Kingdom and glory, instead of remaining hopelessly stuck in the mud of our divisions. Sure, hang on to those convictions that have blessed you; but, at the same time, be an answer to Jesus' World-changing Prayer.

I am not advocating "peace at any price." Some divisions are necessary (1 Cor 11:18-19). This occurs mainly when sin has not been dealt with in the biblical way that Jesus commanded (Matt. 18:15-17). His steps, when followed in love, will preserve unity among those with true faith. But, even in church discipline, we are instructed to discipline in love, always desiring and working for reconciliation (2 Thess 3:13-15).

God's children are to be peaceful, not cantankerous (Rom 12:18; Heb 12:14; 2 Tim 2:22-26). We should be filled with love, which means we will give the other person the benefit of the doubt and live patiently with one another (1 Cor 13:4-7).

The new revelation that Christ had shown Paul was the miracle of Jewish and Gentile unity in Christ. He revealed this to the Ephesians in these words:

"But now in Christ Jesus you who were once far off have been brought near by the blood of Christ. For he himself is our peace, who has made us both (Jew and Gentile) one and has broken down in his flesh the dividing wall of hostility ... that he might create in himself one new man in the place of the two, so making peace...." *(Eph 2:13-15)*

So, Paul powerfully commanded the Ephesians to preserve their unity, urging them to *"walk in a manner worthy of the calling to which you have been called, with all humility and gentleness, with patience, bearing with one another in love, eager to maintain the unity of the Spirit in the bond of peace."* *(Eph 4:1-3).*

Why were they to live so devotedly for unity? Paul immediately explains, *"There is one body and one Spirit ... one Lord, one faith, one baptism, one God and Father of all,*

who is over all, and through all and in all."
(Eph 4:4-6)

It was for this unity in Christ that Jesus prayed so ardently in His Prayer of John 17. Are most divisions worth it? Of course not! They are often produced by sin and grieve the Spirit, Who teaches us in the Word how to deal with our and others sins. So, begin where we can, as brothers and sisters in Christ, with a missional unity informed by the Great Commission and the Spirit-filled examples of the first disciples revealed in the New Testament.

Appendix Three
Time to Start Afresh

We must take seriously today the commands of Jesus to the church at Ephesus. Following their repentance, they were told, **do the works you did at first." (Revelation 2:4)** We have looked briefly at the spirit that marks many believers' initial reception of the Gospel. But Jesus speaks of works that follow the first love union with Christ in our lives. The whole New Testament reveals what followed their first moments of saving faith. The same is emerging within today's Disciple Making Movements (DMMs). But, like the Ephesians, many of us who have been saved, have drifted away from the life we first lived in Christ. And the love that empowered it.

So, here are my 15 humble suggestions to you, my dear friends. These could, by the grace of God, restore our lifestyle as disciples of Jesus. In these ways, I believe we can return to the place of blessing and power, becoming true answers to the Life-Changing Prayer of Jesus:

• Praise the Father for your actual union with Jesus in His death, resurrection, and reign – then live in the power of your union

• Pray with faith the Lord's Prayer (Our Father), thoughtfully, every morning – note, it is not me-centered but our-centered, which makes it an incredibly UNIFYING & GLOBAL prayer

• "Be filled with the Spirit" every morning, and "keep in step" with Him throughout the day – He is our Empowerer (Zech 4:6; Acts 1:8) and Sanctifier (Rom 15:16; 2 Thess 2:13; 1 Pet 1:2)

• Read your Bible (slowly with reflection) each morning and as often as possible (in larger chunks) during the day, as a doer not just a hearer. Memorize it often, starting, perhaps, with the teaching and commands of Jesus in the Gospels

• Commit your works/plans to the Lord, trusting Him to direct your thoughts and path throughout the day (Proverbs 16:3)

• Ask the Father, "What shall I do, Lord" (Acts 22:10) – wait for the response of the Spirit ("still, small voice")– and do it ASAP that day

• Pray specifically for the love of Jesus to flow through you to everyone, starting with your closest family or colleagues – you cannot do this without SMILING, looking at them eye-to-eye

• Do everything "in the name of Jesus" – revealing how you really are abiding and complete in Him = "Pray without ceasing"

• Determine to "not judge" (Matt 7:1-drawing quick conclusions, acting on them) anyone, especially brothers and sisters in Christ; rather, forgive everyone you can (Matt 6:12; Mk 11:25; Eph 4:32)

• Confess to your Father every sin you are convicted of, and forgive others of every offense possible, knowing that "love covers a multitude of sins," always remembering Christ's rule in dealing with sin in Matt. 18:15-17

• Work together with every other true disciple, esteeming them better than yourself, especially the "weaker brethren," serving them rather than demanding them to agree with you (Rom 14:1-23)

• Tell others that you love them and then show that love by helping them, in Christ's name, however you can

• Keep Christ's Matthew 28 Great Commission as your general guideline – Make disciples (the command) by (1) going, (2) baptizing & (3) training by example everyone to obey everything He commanded the disciples to do

• Follow Luke 10:1-16 as your missional model as closely as possible – as literally as possible – PRAY-GO-FIND-DISCIPLE

• Pray that *"the God of peace will sanctify you completely, (so that) your whole spirit, and soul and body be kept blameless to the coming of our Lord Jesus Christ. He who calls you is faithful; he will also surely do it" (1 Thess. 5:23)*